WORD SEARCH
PUZZLES
FOR YOUR BACKPACK

WHAT'S FOR BREAKFAST?

PORRIDGE F A
O M E L E T O A L A
T P A N C A K E
A S B S G I A
R E A E G G U
C H O C O L A

D1607677

ERIC BERLIN

PUZZLE
WRIGHT
JUNIOR

JUNIOR   New York

An Imprint of Sterling Publishing Co., Inc.
1166 Avenue of the Americas
New York, NY 10036

ISBN 978-1-4549-3431-8

Distributed in Canada by Sterling Publishing, Co., Inc.
c/o Canadian Manda Group, 664 Annette Street
Toronto, Ontario M6S 2C8, Canada
Distributed in the United Kingdom by GMC Distribution Services
Castle Place, 166 High Street, Lewes, East Sussex BN7 1XU, England
Distributed in Australia by NewSouth Books
University of New South Wales, Sydney, NSW 2052, Australia

For information about custom editions, special sales, and premium and
corporate purchases, please contact Sterling Special Sales at 800-805-5489
or specialsales@sterlingpublishing.com.

Manufactured in Canada
Lot #:
2 4 6 8 10 9 7 5 3 1
08/19

Cover design by Kristin Logsdon

sterlingpublishing.com
puzzlewright.com

CONTENTS

INTRODUCTION

If you've ever completed a puzzle and said—to somebody in the room or even to yourself—"Hey, look! I did it!," then you already know why puzzles exist. They're here to tease our brains a bit and then make us grin with satisfaction when we finally crack one and reach the answer.

The fun thing about word searches is, they're like a bunch of different puzzles wrapped up into one. You scan the grid, you find one of the words, you give yourself a little pat on the back ... and then you're off to find the next word. Word searches are simple, they're straightforward, and they pack a lot of puzzle satisfaction into a small space. They're some of the first puzzles I ever solved, and they helped make me into the huge puzzle nerd I am today.

If you're new to the puzzle type, here's how they work: I'll give you a grid of letters. In that grid are hidden a whole bunch of words and phrases, all connected by the puzzle's theme. Your job is to find every one of those words or phrases, ignoring any spaces, punctuation, accent marks, or words in parentheses. Each can be found in a straight line, reading up, down, left, right, or diagonally. When you find one, circle it in the grid. Entries will criss-cross and overlap each other in the grid, so in the completed puzzle, certain letters will be circled more than once.

That's the basics of it: Look for a word, find the word, circle the word. But every once in a while, I'm going to throw you a curveball.

- Don't look too hard for the words in the "Opposite Day" word list (page 20)—none of them are in the grid! Instead, you'll need to find an *opposite* of each word.

- In "Two for One" (page 30), every word in the list is missing a letter. You can fill in the blank with two different letters to make two different words—and both those words can be found in the grid.

- There are blanks in the "Name Game" word list, too (page 47). This time, though, you won't be filling in a single letter—you'll need to fill in an entire common name, male or female. For example, given the word P___SE, you'd fill in the name LEA to make PLEASE, and that's the word you'd find in the grid.

- One of the final puzzles in the book is particularly tricky. "Inside Out" (page 64) gives you 19 short words on the left side of the page, and another 19 words on the right. Each of the left-side words can fit inside one of the words on the right, to make a new, longer word or phrase. For example, if I gave you the word LOG, and also the word CONE, you can put the first into the second to make the word COLOGNE—and that's the word you'll need to find.

For any of these puzzles, if you need help knowing what words have been hidden in the puzzle, you can find complete word lists on page 66 or 67.

But wait, we're not done with the curveballs just yet! In a few puzzles—"Can Do!" (page 24), "Traffic Jam" (page 35), and "Slices of Pi" (page 45)—you'll find strange symbols in your word search grid. These are rebuses. In each case, a rebus symbol stands for multiple letters. For example, you'll find little tin cans (🥫) all through the "Can Do!" puzzle. Each one represents the word CAN. So the word TOUCAN would be found in the grid as TOU🥫. Get it?

One more thing: After you've finished circling all the words in a word search, don't rush off to the next puzzle. Instead, take a look at all the letters in the grid that you didn't circle. Read in order from left to right, row by row, they'll spell out a secret message related to that puzzle's theme. It might be a fascinating fact, or a joke, or a riddle you can solve. It's a little bonus—a reward for finding all the words! Hopefully it will make you grin with satisfaction, just like a good puzzle is supposed to do.

Thanks and love to my wife, Janinne, and daughter, Lea, who helped me come up with the puzzle ideas and word lists for this book.

Good luck, and happy hunting!

—Eric Berlin

```
R  E  V  E  L  C  K  A  W  F  U
S  C  I  T  N  A  C  H  N  N  D
Y  U  C  J  G  N  I  K  O  J  R
L  O  O  K  E  M  T  V  M  I  O
U  G  M  I  S  H  S  T  O  S  L
F  C  I  I  R  A  P  U  U  J  L
Y  S  C  E  Y  A  A  O  O  A  U
A  A  A  Y  U  S  L  T  C  O  F
L  A  L  T  J  U  S  I  L  A  H
P  M  U  T  C  O  C  G  H  H  T
C  U  H  I  O  R  C  R  T  Y  R
L  S  D  W  A  O  E  U  S  K  I
N  I  I  F  C  M  K  E  L  C  M
R  N  R  D  R  U  S  B  A  A  O
R  G  G  U  F  H  F  A  W  W  R
```

ABSURD	JOKING
AMUSING	JOVIAL
ANTIC	MIRTHFUL
CLEVER	PLAYFUL
COMICAL	RIDICULOUS
DROLL	SLAPSTICK
FARCICAL	WACKY
HILARIOUS	WHIMSICAL
HUMOROUS	WITTY
JOCULAR	

```
A A O F B R N I M C A
R N I H S U L O G O T
A A R G T E R R B T H
A H C P A O N U D A O
I G Y S C C S H N S G
R G I C A U N E A D U
E A O I I G N F L D I
G A I A P A A A I N N
L I D D O N T D Z H E
A S E A I D U N A R A
I I T K H A M E W M Y
D N R S T C T A S A N
T U E S E C N O L M E
B T B N A D U S I I K
N E A N A W S T O B D
```

ALGERIA	LESOTHO
BOTSWANA	MADAGASCAR
BURKINA FASO	MALI
BURUNDI	MOROCCO
CHAD	RWANDA
EGYPT	SUDAN
ETHIOPIA	SWAZILAND
GABON	TOGO
GHANA	TUNISIA
GUINEA	UGANDA
KENYA	

3 VIDEO GAMES

```
R S T R A T E G Y M Y
A E S R I H C T I W T
E O M O H A L A O G I
D R A O B R E D A E L
O S U S T T A M R E A
C R C T E E D V I E
T N O O N O V E E L R
A S N T V E L R Z A L
E H T E E E V Z U N A
H D R R N S U D R E U
C D O I O P D V A I T
M U L T I P L A Y E R
D N L E O G S A E M I
O E E L O S N O C H V
S S R E T C A R A H C
```

ADVENTURE
BOSS
CHARACTERS
CHEAT CODE
CONSOLE
CONTROLLER
GAME OVER
GOAL
HEADSET
LEADERBOARD

LEVEL
MULTIPLAYER
ONLINE
PUZZLE
REMOTE
SPORTS
STRATEGY
TWITCH
VIRTUAL REALITY

```
T  L  L  I  M  D  A  E  R  T  H
E  H  O  I  D  R  A  C  G  Y  M
E  X  C  E  R  W  A  R  M  U  P
E  C  K  N  I  R  S  E  S  U  B
P  S  E  T  E  E  H  E  N  I  M
A  C  R  B  O  B  D  C  C  A  U
H  I  R  Y  A  M  H  Y  E  S  S
S  B  O  U  N  I  C  B  X  T  C
N  O  O  D  N  L  E  P  E  R  L
I  R  M  G  E  C  U  Z  R  E  E
T  E  B  Z  N  R  H  L  C  N  S
E  A  E  A  S  I  E  E  I  G  X
G  E  L  R  C  A  I  S  S  T  E
T  A  H  E  H  T  L  A  E  H  M
B  S  P  U  H  S  U  P  I  N  D
```

AEROBICS	LOCKER ROOM
BALANCE BEAM	MUSCLES
BENCH	PUNCHING BAG
BICYCLE	PUSH-UPS
CARDIO	STAIR CLIMBER
CRUNCHES	STRENGTH
EXERCISE	TREADMILL
GET IN SHAPE	WARM UP
HEALTH	

SWEET STUFF

```
E  Y  T  I  N  I  V  I  D  A  J
T  I  R  A  M  I  S  U  E  E  D
A  Q  Y  U  G  A  R  R  L  A  T
L  C  E  F  R  U  O  L  E  O  F
O  C  H  T  F  M  O  R  C  H  E
C  O  W  E  S  A  B  N  I  O  A
O  O  R  L  E  R  T  D  N  C  P
H  L  S  S  E  S  U  L  A  U  P
C  W  R  G  G  H  E  D  I  P  L
A  H  N  I  E  M  R  C  L  C  E
R  I  U  I  A  A  S  G  A  A  P
G  P  R  R  T  L  D  O  T  K  I
W  N  A  S  R  L  C  N  I  E  E
I  C  U  N  B  O  R  E  U  A  Z
I  C  E  I  N  W  O  R  B  S  L
```

APPLE PIE	ECLAIR
BROWNIE	GINGERBREAD
CARAMEL	ITALIAN ICE
CHEESECAKE	JELL-O
CHOCOLATE	MARSHMALLOW
CHURRO	NOUGAT
COOL WHIP	S'MORE
CUPCAKE	SUNDAE
CUSTARD	TAFFY
DIVINITY	TIRAMISU

UP THE MOUNTAIN

```
I  I  C  E  A  X  E  F  I  C  H
T  A  K  V  L  E  T  D  L  O  O
E  C  A  L  T  B  I  I  I  M  X
M  X  E  S  I  B  M  A  M  U  Y
L  O  P  T  T  B  U  A  E  R  G
E  N  T  E  U  A  B  Q  R  O  E
H  T  R  E  D  L  U  O  B  C  N
I  N  U  P  E  I  T  I  W  K  S
S  O  U  O  P  L  T  D  E  S  E
P  S  L  M  R  R  I  R  P  P
T  S  E  R  E  V  E  E  O  F  O
E  N  P  N  R  T  S  L  L  N  R
T  O  P  U  R  S  S  E  P  T  H
E  E  A  S  C  A  A  L  X  A  T
O  R  R  G  N  A  H  R  E  V  O
```

ALTITUDE	ICE AXE
BOULDER	OVERHANG
BUTTRESS	OXYGEN
CLIMB	PEAK
EQUIPMENT	RAPPEL
EVEREST	ROCKS
EXPEDITION	ROPES
EXPLORE	ROUTE
GUIDE	SCRAMBLE
HARNESS	SLOPE
HELMET	STEEP

ENGLISH CLASS

```
T  I  B  L  B  R  E  V  D  A  E
N  I  F  I  O  R  E  S  S  A  Y
E  O  D  T  G  E  R  U  N  D  S
S  E  S  E  N  T  E  N  C  E  P
P  L  U  R  A  L  S  E  X  U  T
E  S  C  A  E  E  A  P  N  T  A
L  U  F  T  P  P  N  C  T  E  X
L  B  G  U  A  R  T  C  H  A  A
I  J  S  R  R  U  O  S  T  G  B
N  E  E  E  A  E  N  N  R  N  N
G  C  S  T  G  M  Y  D  I  I  S
P  T  I  U  R  S  M  R  O  D  F
V  O  E  D  A  B  S  A  Y  A  S
N  O  U  N  P  L  C  I  R  E  E
E  S  A  R  H  P  C  N  C  R  E
```

ADVERB	PARAGRAPH
ANTONYMS	PHRASE
CLAUSE	PLURALS
EDIT	PUNCTUATION
ESSAY	READING
FIRST PERSON	SENTENCE
GERUNDS	SPELLING
GRAMMAR	SUBJECT
LITERATURE	SYNTAX
NOUN	TENSE

8 — LET'S MAKE A MOVIE

```
G S N S O L E U Q E S
W R O T C E R I D W S
H R E C U D O R P O I
T S S E R T C A U E E
G W A F N S S N V N T
N H E F F S D I O W R
I A S E T T C H I E N
T F M L R U P R C I A
H L S A L O L E E V M
G E C I R N G X O E T
I K R C T E H T V R N
L A I E N C M R E P U
I M P P M A A A R T T
E D T S M O V S C I S
E S C E N E D I T O R
```

ACTRESS
CAMERAMAN
CAST
DIRECTOR
EDITOR
EXTRAS
GREENSCREEN
LIGHTING
MICROPHONE
PREVIEW

PRODUCER
SCENE
SCORE
SCRIPT
SEQUEL
SOUNDTRACK
SPECIAL EFFECTS
STUNTMAN
VOICEOVER

LA LA LA LA LA!

```
E  G  A  U  G  N  A  L  L  S  N
A  H  C  R  K  O  I  A  I  R  W
D  G  A  E  S  I  S  T  O  I  O
L  U  L  S  C  L  I  D  A  A  D
L  A  A  A  N  G  A  S  A  L  Y
L  L  B  L  N  R  A  G  M  R  A
D  T  B  Y  B  D  S  H  O  L  L
N  S  R  A  R  A  S  T  U  O  G
A  A  L  H  A  I  A  L  G  T  N
L  L  L  A  U  R  N  U  I  R  Y
A  D  S  G  O  E  B  T  E  D  L
L  L  N  B  Y  Y  G  T  H  I  E
A  A  A  N  D  W  N  R  G  O  T
L  L  N  A  T  A  H  E  A  L  A
A  W  L  N  L  L  E  K  A  L  L
```

LABORATORY	LARGE
LABRADOR	LARYNGITIS
LABYRINTH	LASAGNA
LADYBUG	LASER
LAGOON	LASSO
LAKE	LAST LAUGH
LA-LA LAND	LATELY
LANDSLIDE	LATIN
LANGUAGE	LAWYER
LANGUISH	LAY DOWN
LANTERN	

```
E U C E B R A B W E B
C Y N A L U N E H O S
H A L O G C V L A E S
C E A U I T I T S N P
A O S N J T O S F U O
E T F P U N A A P J L
B D U I N L I C D O F
E R A C G K C D A T P
G H E N S C E N U V I
N O U I O O C A S N L
I S D C U M R S T N F
H T I T I M E L R S U
S M M W O A A L O O P
I E S R I H M S H D O
F I R E W O R K S N E
```

AUGUST	JUNE
BARBECUE	LEMONADE
BEACH	PICNIC
BOAT	POOL
FIREWORKS	POPSICLE
FISHING	SAND CASTLE
FLIP-FLOPS	SHORTS
HAMMOCK	SUNGLASSES
HOT DOG	SWIM
ICE CREAM	VACATION
JULY	

```
C T E F X A B S W A T
I A S O T O S A N U A
L T T R O R I N M D H
B S E T U E E B P S N
U O S P L B L S A E O
P P S N D E U D E E L
E G N I W L D L T D L
R N N E L L A R L T A
S I E I E I A O I N G
N D O F O O H S R V N
I A N E W N I C S N E
A R M A D I L L O O T
L T G E Y O C N O R B
P O E D A O R L I A R
N R O H G N O L A R S
```

ARMADILLO	RAILROAD
BOOTS	REBELLION
BRONCO	REPUBLIC
BULL	RODEO
CATTLE DRIVE	SADDLE
CHILI	SPURS
DESERT	TEN-GALLON HAT
FORT	TRADING POST
LASSO	TUMBLEWEED
LONGHORN	WAGON
PLAINS	

IT'S THE LAW

```
L W H Y H T A O Y D I
E D T R U O C T R L Y
S D O H D Y E E U I E
N N A V T E J S J A N
U O L L E U S R U B R
O B I R S R E U E I O
C U T T S A R S C T T
G E I L U D E U I C T
F C G A M C A L L R A
E M A I M E E R P E B
M R T R O I N S M G D
I W I T N E S S O H A
R Y O E S A C T C R O
C C N V E R D I C T P
O U D E G E L L A R T
```

ACCOMPLICE	COURT	OVERRULED
ACCUSED	CRIME	PLEA
ALLEGED	GUILTY	PROSECUTION
ATTORNEY	JURY	SUIT
BAIL	JUSTICE	SUMMONS
BOND	LITIGATION	TRIAL
CASE	OATH	VERDICT
COUNSEL	OBJECT	WITNESS

The words in the list below aren't in the grid—their opposites are!
For the full list of opposites, see page 66.

```
W H T N A N O S N O C
Y A T I T T A P A I H
R S O N F N O R P O P
E O I N S U E I R T E
N X S O A L R I L O E
O F P C N B Z I T O W
I U R E S O Q L E A O
T T Y N N U S T N R P
S E R T I S C C W E E
E T A D C O I C R B N
U L U D R E S V E M T
Q L A D N E L H E E A
T A B T E O V L T M D
H T E N S N D E A E I
N S L A R U T A N R T
```

ALWAYS
ANSWER
ARTIFICIAL
ATTIC
CHEAP
CLOSED
CLOUDY
DOCTOR
FAIL
FORGET
FRESH

GUILTY
QUIET
SHARP
SHORT
SOLID
TEACHER
VERTICAL
VOWEL
WIDE
YOUNG

HAIL TO THE CHIEF

```
T  S  E  Y  A  H  H  E  W  H  N
R  T  L  E  V  E  S  O  O  R  E
I  O  N  T  N  A  M  U  R  T  R
E  N  L  A  H  O  A  U  B  E  U
S  E  O  Y  N  M  D  W  W  A  B
S  O  N  T  A  A  A  O  N  C  N
D  N  L  B  G  T  H  E  T  C  A
N  H  O  K  A  N  E  C  A  L  V
A  A  C  S  E  R  I  R  U  G  E
L  P  N  S  R  N  T  H  S  B  T
E  I  I  H  O  E  N  U  S  S  E
V  E  L  I  R  N  F  E  A  A  M
E  R  O  M  L  L  I  F  D  E  W
L  C  L  I  N  T  O  N  E  Y  R
C  E  O  R  N  O  M  I  C  J  A
```

ADAMS	LINCOLN
BUCHANAN	MONROE
BUSH	OBAMA
CARTER	PIERCE
CLEVELAND	REAGAN
CLINTON	ROOSEVELT
EISENHOWER	TAYLOR
FILLMORE	TRUMAN
HAYES	VAN BUREN
JEFFERSON	WASHINGTON
KENNEDY	

PARTY FAVORS

```
Y  O  R  I  B  B  O  N  P  U  R
R  M  E  S  L  I  M  E  O  E  M
W  T  S  N  A  S  A  N  K  D  K
D  A  A  A  I  N  D  A  W  C  C
K  T  R  I  U  A  M  L  U  H  L
C  T  E  T  B  E  H  R  O  E  C
I  O  S  H  S  B  T  C  A  P  H
T  O  S  I  P  Y  O  P  Y  T  A
S  S  O  D  O  L  Z  L  Y  E  L
W  N  A  T  A  L  B  A  A  L  K
O  I  O  T  O  E  U  Y  R  E  T
L  S  E  Y  T  J  B  D  A  C  H
G  I  E  N  A  O  I  O  I  A  S
E  A  G  N  I  R  M  H  T  R  A
K  R  E  P  E  N  C  I  L  B  R
```

BEADS	PEANUTS
BRACELET	PENCIL
CHALK	PLAY-DOH
CHOCOLATE	RAISINS
CRAYONS	RIBBON
CRAZY STRAW	RING
ERASER	SLIME
GLOWSTICK	TATTOO
JELLY BEANS	TIARA
KEYCHAIN	TOY TRUCK
NOISEMAKER	

YELLOW THINGS

```
T  R  H  E  L  C  T  O  L  O  S
R  Y  E  E  B  E  L  B  M  U  B
D  E  M  W  L  L  L  O  B  W  S
A  O  I  E  O  S  A  L  S  N  P
N  C  M  E  S  L  O  O  O  W  O
D  O  C  L  C  O  F  S  K  A  N
E  R  K  K  H  A  P  N  C  R  G
L  N  I  C  A  M  N  T  U  T  E
I  E  S  U  I  D  W  A  D  S  G
O  I  T  S  X  H  H  C  R  O  G
N  U  E  Y  A  R  C  A  E  Y  Y
G  H  E  E  T  I  N  Y  B  J  O
T  M  I  N  I  O  N  S  B  A  L
L  I  D  O  F  F  A  D  U  A  K
P  A  C  H  E  E  S  E  R  N  B
```

BABY CHICK	MINIONS
BUMBLEBEE	OMELET
CANARY	RUBBER DUCK
CHEESE	SCHOOL BUS
CORN	SPONGE
DAFFODIL	STRAW
DANDELION	SUNFLOWER
EGG YOLK	TAXI
HONEYSUCKLE	THE SIMPSONS
LEMON	

CAN DO!

Each entry in this puzzle contains the word CAN, and in the grid, the letters C-A-N are represented by an image of a can.

```
A  K  C  I  T  S  E  L  D  🥫  A
G  R  A  N  D  🥫  Y  O  N  F  🥫
🥫  A  🥫  D  I  N  A  G  R  S  E
U  A  I  R  O  E  O  I  🥫  S  P
O  E  R  O  I  R  🥫  D  N  A  U
T  U  E  Y  🥫  V  A  N  🥫  T  O
H  O  M  E  I  L  🥫  A  🥫  N  L
T  O  A  O  S  S  O  I  T  A  A
O  R  L  B  🥫  E  L  V  🥫  E  T
L  E  L  X  E  P  P  A  E  C  🥫
T  E  A  T  P  E  M  N  N  🥫  D
🥫  🥫  T  A  O  A  D  I  E  D  A
A  C  N  🥫  N  O  N  D  E  Y  S
V  U  C  A  E  T  H  🥫  T  🥫  E
🥫  B  P  E  L  I  🥫  S  🥫  E  🥫
```

AFRICAN VIOLET	HURRICANE
ALL-AMERICAN	PANAMA CANAL
APPLICANT	PECANS
BUCCANEER	PELICAN
CANARY ISLANDS	SCANDAL
CANDLESTICK	SCANDINAVIAN
CANDY CANE	SCANNER
CANNON	TOUCAN
CANTALOUPE	VACANT LOT
CANTEEN	VOLCANO
GRAND CANYON	

18 HEY U

```
W H A Y T I L I T U T
M T U A L M U W A O U
U U R K I D M U E M N
I N P E U P P A B N I
N R C H I L O R P N Q
A O G L O C E T U H U
R C A A E L S L U E E
U I D U L Y S S E S E
M N B A C E C T R A O
P U M E Y S A E E C E
T A R H C M V A N R D
E B A A I I G W I E Y
E H E T N N Y P O P U
N C L U U M U T P O
N U E L A U S U N U U
```

UKULELE
ULTIMATE
ULYSSES
UMBRELLA
UMLAUT
UMPIRE
UMPTEEN
UNCLE
UNICORN
UNICYCLE
UNIQUE

UNIVERSE
UNUSUAL
UPBEAT
UPHOLSTERY
UPLOAD
UPPERCASE
URANIUM
URANUS
UTILITY
UTOPIA

BIG TIME

```
S  C  I  T  N  A  G  I  G  I  S
Y  U  N  R  E  P  U  S  T  I  V
S  T  O  E  T  A  E  G  R  A  L
B  U  F  M  E  V  I  S  S  A  M
I  S  O  E  R  T  O  T  I  O  D
M  U  D  N  H  O  T  T  N  H  E
A  O  T  D  I  E  N  D  L  V  I
C  G  N  O  G  A  O  E  I  T  E
O  N  T  U  T  L  T  S  E  G  S
L  O  H  S  M  I  S  N  I  S  N
O  M  B  A  B  E  I  A  U  G  E
S  U  G  M  R  E  N  R  W  O  M
S  H  O  P  U  T  R  T  D  T  M
A  H  M  A  N  J  B  I  A  G  I
L  I  L  U  F  I  T  N  E  L  P
```

COLOSSAL	LARGE
ENORMOUS	MASSIVE
GIANT	MONDO
GIGANTIC	MONUMENTAL
HEFTY	MOUNTAINOUS
HUGE	PLENTIFUL
HUMONGOUS	SUBSTANTIAL
IMMENSE	SUPER
IMPRESSIVE	TREMENDOUS
JUMBO	VAST

BUG TIME

```
A  B  O  T  I  U  Q  S  O  M  R
G  E  A  E  B  S  W  K  Y  A  I
N  N  G  G  U  A  C  S  L  D  E
G  B  I  I  T  N  L  F  R  D
E  E  A  W  T  T  I  T  E  A  E
A  E  L  R  E  P  M  O  S  G  P
S  T  B  A  R  C  T  K  U  O  I
A  W  O  E  F  H  A  U  O  N  T
D  N  T  D  L  T  A  L  H  F  N
A  A  R  E  Y  B  E  E  T  L  E
C  E  D  D  K  T  M  I  L  Y  C
I  M  I  E  S  C  E  U  A  F  C
C  D  W  E  E  V  I  L  B  H  S
E  Y  L  F  T  I  U  R  F  C  O
N  D  H  C  A  O  R  K  C  O  C
```

ANTS	EARWIG
BEETLE	FLEA
BUMBLEBEE	FRUIT FLY
BUTTERFLY	GNAT
CATERPILLAR	HOUSEFLY
CENTIPEDE	KATYDID
CICADA	LACEWING
COCKROACH	MOSQUITO
CRICKET	TICK
DRAGONFLY	WEEVIL

WORLD CAPITALS

```
B  T  O  K  Y  O  D  J  O  E  W
S  E  D  I  R  D  A  M  T  A  C
H  E  R  I  B  K  W  A  S  A  O
S  H  A  L  A  E  I  H  R  N  P
Q  C  Y  R  I  G  I  A  T  R  E
O  U  T  N  P  N  C  J  A  O  N
S  A  I  T  G  A  O  G  I  F  H
F  I  C  T  S  C  U  E  O  N  A
N  L  O  Y  O  E  D  I  R  E  G
A  N  C  T  L  I  V  B  I  E  E
N  R  I  C  T  A  P  O  Y  I  N
A  T  X  A  W  A  S  R  A  W  L
V  I  E  N  N  A  W  I  D  L  E
A  T  M  A  N  I  L  A  H  T  E
H  R  O  G  A  I  T  N  A  S  S
```

BEIJING (China)	NAIROBI (Kenya)
BERLIN (Germany)	OTTAWA (Canada)
CAIRO (Egypt)	PRAGUE (The Czech Republic)
CARACAS (Venezuela)	QUITO (Ecuador)
COPENHAGEN (Denmark)	RIYADH (Saudi Arabia)
HAVANA (Cuba)	SANTIAGO (Chile)
JAKARTA (Indonesia)	TOKYO (Japan)
MADRID (Spain)	VIENNA (Austria)
MANILA (The Philippines)	WARSAW (Poland)
MEXICO CITY (Mexico)	WASHINGTON (The U.S.)

CAMPING TRIP

```
F F O S O M R E H T R
A L C C O M P A S S L
L O A T R E T A E H T
A O B S F C P E O I T
K F I S H I N G K S P
E E N E L L E D E C A
W R T M R L I R P K B
I U U I N A O G R G A
L T I T T F W A H S C
D A A S N R P K N T K
L N R I N E A T O E P
I I E N T T V I T O A
F S E A X A P D L N C
E E T R I W E N A A K
C S R O O D T U O C E
```

ADVENTURE	HATCHET
BACKPACK	HEATER
CABIN	LAKE
CANOE	NATURE
COMPASS	OUTDOORS
COOKWARE	STATE PARK
FIRST-AID KIT	THERMOS
FISHING	TRAIL
FLASHLIGHT	WATERFALL
FOREST	WILDLIFE

TWO FOR ONE

You can fill in each blank below with two different letters, making two different words. Each of those words is hiding in the grid. For the full list of words, see page 66.

```
T  R  E  C  N  O  C  N  A  M  D
O  L  I  O  P  S  T  A  T  U  E
R  E  T  H  G  U  A  L  E  T  V
R  H  T  N  A  S  A  E  L  P  O
A  E  T  A  N  A  T  N  U  S  U
C  W  R  O  V  L  O  O  P  S  R
A  W  N  E  I  I  M  A  S  L  E
T  S  H  L  T  T  R  U  P  N  P
N  H  A  I  T  H  T  P  R  O  S
A  S  D  M  M  A  G  E  I  I  I
S  U  E  I  T  P  C  U  M  T  H
A  L  T  S  E  N  E  P  A  I  W
E  T  O  N  O  D  L  R  T  D  I
H  A  U  C  N  E  O  N  E  D  K
P  N  R  E  Y  T  O  R  R  A  P
```

A _ DITION	PRI _ ATE
_ ARROT	SIM _ LE
_ AUGHTER	SPO _ L
CONCER _	STATU _
DE _ OUR	SU _ TAN
P _ EASANT	WHI _ PER

NAVAL GAZING

```
R R A D A R M W H P F
Y E A T H N D L A O L
A I D W O B C T E A I
B R E D Y T R H R H G
K R H E U O F I O O H
C A S L L R M K D R T
I C S T C D I P O G D
S N T H A E O N M K E
N A V R P R Y P M C C
R G A E T G B W O O K
F E I H A A E O C D R
R T O S I L O R A Y E
A L T F N L O P R R L
E U N T E E L F C D D
H T N E M Y O L P E D
```

AHOY
ANCHOR
BRIDGE
CAPTAIN
CARRIER
COMMODORE
CREW
DEPLOYMENT
DRY DOCK
ENSIGN
FLEET

FLIGHT DECK
GALLEY
HELM
PATROL
PORTHOLE
PROW
RADAR
REAR ADMIRAL
RUDDER
SICK BAY
STARBOARD

MUSICAL INSTRUMENTS

```
D  N  O  I  D  R  O  C  C  A  W
H  R  L  I  C  R  L  D  H  B  I
T  B  O  Y  E  A  U  M  I  U  A
N  U  T  H  R  L  B  M  H  T  C
I  G  P  I  C  E  A  S  S  L  I
I  L  N  I  S  I  S  T  E  S  N
C  E  M  O  C  N  S  N  N  T  O
T  E  N  R  O  C  O  P  I  E  M
R  V  T  G  A  H  O  I  R  N  R
N  S  I  N  P  A  N  L  U  A  A
N  I  L  O  D  N  A  M  O  T  H
S  A  L  G  L  E  C  E  B  S  O
N  Y  G  D  I  I  O  N  M  A  S
X  T  R  R  U  B  N  M  A  C  E
R  E  D  R  O  C  E  R  T  N  T
```

ACCORDION	LYRE
BASSOON	MANDOLIN
BUGLE	OBOE
CASTANETS	ORGAN
CLARINET	PICCOLO
CORNET	RECORDER
DRUMS	TAMBOURINE
DULCIMER	TUBA
GONG	VIOLIN
HARMONICA	XYLOPHONE
HARPSICHORD	

26 A CHEESY PUZZLE

```
Y N A C I R E M A O U
C A T N S D T E A N L
L G T Y A T O S A U R
T T O M S W I S S F R
R I C R R A E L C I O
E S I B G M G O T E M
B L R O R O L N D O A
M I S A U B N T Z H N
E T P D Y P A Z T E O
M D A A E M A I O S M
A A D E R R B N A L C
C G M U E N S T E R A
E N O L O V O R P E K
W A L A T N E M M E R
R A D I T R A V A H S
```

AMERICAN
ASIAGO
BRIE
CAMEMBERT
COLBY
EDAM
EMMENTAL
GOAT
GORGONZOLA
GOUDA
GRUYÈRE

HAVARTI
MOZZARELLA
MUENSTER
PANEER
PARMESAN
PROVOLONE
RICOTTA
ROMANO
STILTON
SWISS
TILSIT

BODIES OF WATER

```
A I R O T C I V T E H
E K M O I H U R O N N
O N I T S C S H O A I
E A C Y O I A N E E A
T R F T N T T B R N L
A I A N Q A B U A A P
I G T L R I G I T R M
M N T I R R Y N L R A
N I O A C D P C A E H
A R C O N A T K N T C
I E A H C I C A T I I
P B N I I A E A I D T
S S F N L G O R C E L
A I W B E A A T I M A
C E L A R O C N R E B
```

<table>
<tr><td>Lakes</td><td>Oceans</td><td>Seas</td></tr>
<tr><td>CHAMPLAIN</td><td>ARCTIC</td><td>ADRIATIC</td></tr>
<tr><td>ERIE</td><td>ATLANTIC</td><td>AEGEAN</td></tr>
<tr><td>HURON</td><td>PACIFIC</td><td>BALTIC</td></tr>
<tr><td>MICHIGAN</td><td></td><td>BERING</td></tr>
<tr><td>ONTARIO</td><td></td><td>BLACK</td></tr>
<tr><td>TAHOE</td><td></td><td>CARIBBEAN</td></tr>
<tr><td>TANGANYIKA</td><td></td><td>CASPIAN</td></tr>
<tr><td>TITICACA</td><td></td><td>CORAL</td></tr>
<tr><td>VICTORIA</td><td></td><td>MEDITERRANEAN</td></tr>
</table>

TRAFFIC JAM

Each entry in this puzzle contains the word CAR, and in the grid, the letters C-A-R are represented by an image of a car.

```
S  U  O  I  🚗 E  R  P  W  H  N
E  L  A  V  I  N  🚗 N  A  O  🚗
E  S  🚗 O  L  E  A  F  R  P  A
R  N  O  🚗 H  G  S  T  E  🚗 T
🚗 S  🚗 I  C  B  H  N  I  T  🚗
S  U  R  N  U  🚗 T  E  A  O  A
A  🚗 A  A  O  E  O  C  K  S  N
G  I  A  L  R  C  Y  U  S  🚗 G
A  🚗 I  M  G  D  I  D  S  L  A
D  N  O  W  E  N  🚗 L  D  E  M
A  I  O  🚗 H  L  E  D  I  T  L
M  V  S  S  T  I  C  T  L  H  G
U  O  B  I  🚗 T  O  O  N  I  C
E  R  M  A  S  🚗 A  T  R  T  W
O  E  I  N  O  🚗 A  M  A  N  D
```

CARAMEL CORN	MACARONI
CARIBOU	MADAGASCAR
CARNATION	MAGNA CARTA
CARNIVAL	MASCARA
CARNIVORE	NORTH CAROLINA
CAROUSEL	OCARINA
CARPENTER	OSCAR THE GROUCH
CARTOON	PRECARIOUS
CHILI CON CARNE	SCAREDY-CAT
ESCAROLE	SCARLET
ICARUS	WILD CARD

OVERWATCH

```
T  H  E  G  O  H  D  A  O  R  G
A  M  O  R  I  S  A  P  E  S  E
P  E  D  N  C  I  A  A  L  D  O
G  H  R  U  U  E  I  Y  A  S  R
R  A  A  O  L  M  V  L  A  E  I
E  M  E  R  C  Y  B  O  P  L  A
I  B  L  D  A  N  Z  A  R  Y  A
N  E  I  N  O  H  E  D  N  S  D
H  T  T  G  W  R  E  T  Y  I  N
A  A  A  L  E  V  A  M  L  O  O
R  R  N  E  D  N  M  D  I  O  M
D  K  E  I  F  E  J  T  O  F  M
T  N  H  E  T  R  S  I  E  N  A
T  U  T  R  L  A  A  N  G  U  H
A  J  A  R  B  M  O  S  G  E  S
```

ATHENA	NUMBANI
BASTION	ORISA
DORADO	PAYLOAD
DRAGONBLADE	PHARAH
GENJI	REAPER
HAMMOND	REINHARDT
JUNKRAT	ROADHOG
LUCIO	SOMBRA
MERCY	SYMMETRA
MOLTEN CORE	ZARYA

ELEGANT NIGHT OUT

```
S  S  D  O  T  F  O  Y  R  T  U
N  G  E  T  I  U  S  R  E  L  R
T  P  N  V  E  L  X  L  L  A  A
E  U  E  I  O  P  R  E  E  M  S
T  S  C  S  R  L  U  W  D  R  C
E  S  K  G  E  R  G  E  T  O  O
P  E  L  N  L  N  A  J  K  F  T
R  R  A  D  I  R  E  E  S  A  S
A  D  C  N  M  L  E  D  O  U  M
C  P  E  T  O  O  F  C  A  F  O
D  V  T  L  U  D  T  F  T  A  R
E  E  L  N  S  S  R  D  U  N  P
R  A  R  A  I  T  T  I  W  C  H
B  E  C  A  N  R  Y  O  A  Y  S
T  A  W  L  E  B  G  A  L  H  L
```

ASCOT	JEWELRY
BALL	LIMOUSINE
CUFFLINKS	MAKEUP
DRESS UP	NECKLACE
EARRINGS	PROM
EVENING WEAR	RED CARPET
FANCY	SUIT
FORMAL	TIARA
GLOVES	TUXEDO
GOWN	WAISTCOAT
HAIRDO	

GEARS OF GOVERNMENT

```
A C R E T S I G E R A
L N D C I R U N O F F
D S D A S E A T T E M
E E S R P N A D O U X
R T M N E N T V D N O
M A E O E I S N E E B
A G P S C W E D N T T
N E E R H R T W S E O
N L E A E K A E K E L
V E R F S S D C S N L
O D E T W O I R Y I A
T R U A N T D D F M B
I E L O R O N F E O F
N M R O F T A L P N I
G C E M R E C O U N T
```

ALDERMAN	REFERENDUM
BALLOT BOX	REGISTER
CANDIDATES	RUNOFF
DELEGATES	SENATOR
DEMOCRACY	SPEECHES
LAWS	TERM
NOMINEE	TICKET
PLATFORM	VETO
PRESIDENT	VOTING
RACE	WINNERS
RECOUNT	

TALENT SHOW

```
E  C  N  A  D  P  A  T  W  M  C
E  M  U  T  S  O  C  O  I  N  G
G  A  T  R  A  T  S  C  N  K  Y
D  G  S  A  O  U  R  W  N  R  S
U  I  I  O  P  O  N  E  E  A  S
J  C  U  A  P  P  B  C  R  T  I
B  I  Q  H  L  U  L  N  N  I  N
E  A  O  N  A  I  P  A  R  U  G
S  N  L  I  B  B  T  M  U  G  E
E  O  I  L  N  S  P  R  I  S  R
Z  N  R  W  E  O  R  O  D  S  E
I  E  T  T  A  T  R  F  E  C  S
R  H  N  S  O  L  V  R  I  T  T
P  O  E  N  A  I  D  E  M  O  C
C  N  V  G  R  E  P  P  A  R  A
```

ACTS	PERFORMANCE
APPLAUSE	PIANO
BALLET	POET
COMEDIAN	PRIZES
CONTESTANTS	RAPPER
COSTUME	SINGER
GUITAR	SKIT
JUDGE	TAP DANCE
MAGICIAN	VENTRILOQUIST
MICROPHONE	WINNER

```
E I F S R E P P I L S
N Y O A R E M A C U H
O O P M A H S C A A N
H M T A C S U L I O T
P A S J E C N R Y N I
U E O A U A B R A S K
E R H P U R L R I T Y
K C C S U F O A S S R
A G E S A D C Y E K T
M N H O O W K O U C E
V I S E I T H E O O L
V V D E R S P T A S I
P A S S P O R T U C O
K H S U R B H T O O T
E S D E N I C I D E M
```

CAMERA	SHAMPOO
DEODORANT	SHAVING CREAM
HAIRBRUSH	SHOES
MAKEUP	SLIPPERS
MEDICINE	SOCKS
MOUTHWASH	SUNBLOCK
PAJAMAS	TIES
PASSPORT	TOILETRY KIT
PHONE	TOOTHBRUSH
SCARF	

SUIT YOU TO A T

```
T  W  H  T  A  T  E  L  B  A  T
T  H  T  T  S  W  O  T  O  R  T
A  L  W  A  I  E  N  P  D  E  O
O  N  O  A  T  A  H  H  A  I  S
B  T  L  B  R  I  R  C  S  E  T
G  M  A  E  R  T  H  T  Y  E  T
U  T  L  O  T  E  A  N  S  O  S
T  O  O  F  R  E  D  N  E  T  T
T  P  T  S  O  H  M  N  S  T  A
L  S  P  T  P  S  T  E  U  S  T
L  E  M  F  E  E  P  A  F  H  T
T  C  E  E  L  M  E  R  I  I  T
Y  R  T  H  E  I  O  R  U  R  D
T  E  X  T  T  S  R  O  T  P
T  T  H  E  T  T  E  E  W  T  S
```

TABLET	THUNDERBOLT
TEACHER'S PET	THWART
TEAPOT	TIMESHEET
TELEPORT	TOAST
TEMPEST	TOLERANT
TEMPT	TOP SECRET
TENDERFOOT	TOY CHEST
TEXT	TRAIT
THEFT	T-SHIRT
THIRST	TUGBOAT
THROAT	TWEET

HOLD EVERYTHING!

```
R  E  H  C  T  I  P  A  N  A  N
F  N  T  E  K  S  A  B  I  A  M
A  I  L  S  T  H  E  A  C  T  B
R  H  L  S  A  T  C  H  E  L  O
A  E  S  E  A  F  S  P  C  K  T
O  U  N  C  C  A  E  C  O  H  T
G  L  I  I  R  A  S  O  C  B  L
A  U  A  T  A  A  B  L  L  A  E
B  N  E  R  J  T  T  I  D  R  S
R  C  A  E  E  T  N  E  N  R  A
E  H  M  K  I  L  R  O  A  E  C
P  B  C  C  K  U  O  U  C  L  T
A  O  R  O  O  A  S  O  N  U  I
P  X  P  L  O  V  I  A  C  K  U
L  E  S  A  C  F  E  I  R  B  S
```

BARREL	LUNCH BOX
BASKET	PAPER BAG
BOTTLE	PITCHER
BRIEFCASE	POCKETBOOK
CHEST	SAFE
CONTAINER	SATCHEL
COOKIE JAR	SUITCASE
COOLER	TRASH CAN
CRATE	TRUNK
FILE CABINET	VAULT
LOCKER	

RAINFOREST ANIMALS

```
L E R O T A G I L L A
T M A R B O C E L O T
U R P R R S A R C T H
H E E I G U A N A K T
O U L E R T N B E L O
J L M L F A E Y E E L
A F O M U R N N Z O S
G R D I I A O H N P P
U N U P T N H G A A A
A E M M O T G C P R R
R A O H E U U B M D R
V E T N T L R Y I Y O
O Y G F M A A A H R T
P D A I G N A S C C D
A R N A T U G N A R O
```

ALLIGATOR
ARMY ANT
CHIMPANZEE
COBRA
GECKO
GORILLA
HUMMINGBIRD
IGUANA
JAGUAR
LEMUR
LEOPARD

OCELOT
ORANGUTAN
PARROT
PIRANHA
PYTHON
SLOTH
TARANTULA
TIGER
TREE FROG
VAMPIRE BAT

37 ALL AROUND THE TOWN

```
A E S U O H E R I F N
D N P O T S S U B I F
M Y O O U C U H L I S
V U E L H I O N A U P
N C I O A T H I P T O
E Y O N E S T E A D H
E L D L I B R A R Y S
R A L G F M U I C T E
G E O A A A O U A P E
N Y T R H L C D E H F
W R K A O Y I T N F F
O E D G E U T S O O O
T K K E M H Y I S R C
C A R A L P T E C R Y
S B D L E I F L L A B
```

BAKERY
BALL FIELD
BUS STOP
CITY HALL
COFFEE SHOP
CONDOMINIUM
COURTHOUSE
DELI
FACTORY
FIREHOUSE

GARAGE
HAIR SALON
HOTEL
LIBRARY
SCHOOL
STADIUM
SUPERMARKET
THEATER
TOWN GREEN

SLICES OF PI

Each entry in this puzzle contains the word PI, and in the grid, the letters P-I are represented by the pi symbol (π).

```
E  C  N  E  F  T  E  K  C  π  C
S  W  E  H  I  S  Y  O  A  V  A
E  E  N  R  C  C  L  π  A  E  π
π  L  π  A  E  Y  C  R  C  U  T
P  S  π  L  M  A  T  E  N  A  A
U  N  E  π  π  R  π  P  O  D  L
G  π  C  T  R  R  E  π  I  π  A
S  S  A  π  E  S  A  D  N  O  T
E  T  C  T  W  π  O  E  π  Q  π
R  Z  S  O  O  N  A  π  O  S  S
π  A  I  I  R  P  I  Z  U  A  O
M  D  H  S  P  π  R  R  Z  I  H
U  T  L  L  T  L  O  I  π  π  O
E  N  E  D  I  N  G  N  I  S  T
S  S  U  O  I  C  π  S  U  S  A
```

ASPIRIN	PIED PIPER
CAPITAL	PINEAPPLE
EMPIRE	PINT-SIZE
ESCAPING	PIZZA PIE
ETHIOPIA	SCORPION
GUPPIES	SEPIA
HOSPITAL	SPIDER-MAN
MASTERPIECE	SPIRIT
OLYMPICS	SUSPICIOUS
OPINION	TYPICAL
PICKET FENCE	UMPIRES

39 SOUTHERN FOOD

```
A E I P S S E H C L A
L A E T T E E W S R G
E I K Y I S G F T S S
E R A V R I N R N G E
H M C T G G I I G E I
S O T F X F D E U L P
I Y E G L O D D M G P
F U V E M E U C B O U
T B L A L B P H O R P
A O E I R R A I K F H
C I V A I G N C R I S
S E D C N A A K A L U
D J E U M S N E B I H
S H R I M P A N O H G
U M B R E L B B O C O
```

BANANA PUDDING	GUMBO
BEANS	HUSH PUPPIES
CATFISH	OKRA
CHESS PIE	OXTAIL
CHILI	RED VELVET CAKE
COBBLER	RICE
DEVILED EGGS	SHRIMP
FRIED CHICKEN	SWEET TEA
FROG LEGS	TRIFLE
GRAVY	YAMS
GRITS	

NAME GAME

Each of these words can be completed by inserting a common three-letter name into the blank. Can you figure out all of the words and then find them in the grid? For the complete word list, see page 67.

```
T  N  A  S  A  E  L  P  Y  O  V
U  E  C  A  N  A  W  A  K  E  N
Y  T  L  A  Y  O  R  N  G  D  T
I  R  V  P  I  C  Y  E  D  E  N
T  H  A  E  M  H  T  A  W  P  E
O  R  R  S  D  A  M  E  R  L  D
T  E  E  D  R  M  S  O  I  C  I
S  E  S  I  D  E  B  U  R  N  S
U  D  A  N  L  L  V  T  O  T  E
O  N  T  G  E  E  L  I  H  W  R
L  I  A  M  O  O  L  G  N  O  T
U  E  H  R  N  N  I  A  Y  N  E
B  R  E  D  L  L  E  A  H  T  A
A  T  O  E  E  R  M  N  A  W  M
F  N  E  D  E  B  A  F  O  S  S
```

_____IVERSARY	FABU_____S	_____ALTY
AWA_____	LON_____	_____PLE
_____GLES	_____OR	SI_____URNS
CHAME_____N	P_____SANT	SOF_____D
C_____ONS	P_____LEM	VEGET_____AN
D_____GHTS	REIN_____R	W_____E
	RE_____ENT	

INTO THE VOLCANO

```
F  U  J  I  O  E  K  O  M  S  N
E  I  A  O  T  A  K  A  R  K  O
A  F  S  J  B  U  V  E  P  I  C
C  R  U  S  T  S  Y  A  T  A  E
I  P  S  R  U  A  I  S  L  M  E
L  R  N  O  L  R  O  D  N  R  M
I  E  E  O  S  H  E  A  I  S  A
S  S  L  O  I  R  V  F  E  A  U
R  S  E  I  A  T  F  O  C  N  N
P  U  H  E  T  O  P  T  H  E  A
L  R  T  A  G  A  I  U  T  U  L
U  E  N  N  N  V  L  L  R  D  O
M  T  I  R  E  E  O  O  D  E  A
E  R  A  V  O  M  L  C  V  A  N
O  E  S  U  I  V  U  S  E  V  S
```

ACTIVE	MOLTEN
CALDERA	OBSIDIAN
CRUST	PLUME
ERUPTION	PRESSURE
ETNA	RING OF FIRE
FISSURE	SAINT HELENS
FUJI	SILICA
KRAKATOA	SMOKE
LAVA	VESUVIUS
LAYERS	VOLATILE
MAUNA LOA	

GLASS ACT

```
T R A J N O S A M I F
Y E O Q U E C D A R P
N A S N U A A I A A N
C M A T R A K R P E E
O O I A T N R E G W B
R I F I G U R I N E O
N E N F D W B L U O L
A E W R E K A E B M G
M S O I D E S D T S W
E H G N I E T N E I O
N H N Y S O U A P R N
T A V N H I S H B P S
S S E A E Y G C O L U
R L G L S A S N S C E
L A Y R L E W E J S S
```

AQUARIUM
BEADS
BEAKER
CARAFE
CHANDELIER
COFFEE TABLE
DISHES
FIGURINE
JEWELRY

LENSES
MASON JAR
NEON SIGN
ORNAMENTS
PAPERWEIGHT
PRISM
SNOW GLOBE
TEST TUBE
VASE

WOW!

```
R E W O M N W A L W A
L N R E U K O W T O W
W W S E R S R W S A R
L O K T O E E T E E E
O D R D R A W K W A W
W W D R H E O O D W O
T O A E A T L E L W T
Y H R T W B F G I F R
T S R O W Y L L W W E
N A I O T O L E F O T
E R N W W O A W E I A
W S N W W A W T E H W
T W O D N I W E R N W
T R O W O L L A W S W
M A W A L K W A Y N E
```

AWKWARD
GLOWWORM
KOWTOW
LAWN MOWER
NEWLYWED
SHOWDOWN
SNOW BLOWER
SWALLOW
THROWAWAY

TWENTY-TWO
WALKWAY
WALLFLOWER
WATER TOWER
WEREWOLF
WHEELBARROW
WILD WEST
WILLOW
WINDOW

```
N  I  L  R  E  B  O  H  A  D  R
V  W  I  A  Y  R  D  N  A  N  N
W  C  O  A  A  S  A  R  T  O  R
E  Y  H  T  L  Y  T  E  T  L  E
F  T  B  I  E  M  R  E  S  L  T
T  S  C  L  O  G  C  O  L  E  S
W  R  S  U  O  N  R  C  N  M  E
N  E  T  L  I  C  A  O  E  E  W
W  H  L  R  G  L  T  R  E  I  H
O  M  P  L  T  R  E  N  I  G  T
R  A  N  E  E  T  H  E  E  R  R
B  U  C  D  M  S  N  L  I  N  O
T  H  A  E  D  O  L  L  S  R  N
S  M  I  T  H  T  R  E  A  A  T
E  N  A  L  U  T  E  Y  Y  C  S
```

AMHERST	NOTRE DAME
BROWN	OBERLIN
CALTECH	PRINCETON
CARNEGIE MELLON	RICE
COLBY	SMITH
CORNELL	TULANE
DARTMOUTH	WELLESLEY
EMORY	WESLEYAN
GEORGETOWN	YALE
NORTHWESTERN	

WELCOME TO MY CASTLE

```
H C R A N O M O A T W
H S R O Y A L T Y N Y
E N H C M Y R O N O H
H A P I L R L E U E N
C S R A E D A R G G E
H E I E L L M D M N G
I L N T O A D A L U D
V B C O J R C L A D I
A O E E R E A E E F R
L N S I G H S H R E B
R T S T T T T T H W
Y Y D A L S E P E L A
K I E N U G E P U R R
T R U O P C H R I A D
G S J D S U K E C E S
```

ARMOR	HONOR	PALACE
CHIVALRY	JESTER	PRINCESS
CREST	JOUST	REALM
DRAWBRIDGE	LADY	ROYALTY
DUNGEON	MOAT	SCEPTER
EARL	MONARCH	SHIELD
GREAT HALL	NOBLES	THRONE
HERALDRY		YOUR MAJESTY

OFFICE SUPPLIES

```
W  H  A  S  R  E  N  O  T  L  S
E  P  A  T  R  T  P  M  A  L  D
S  D  N  A  B  R  E  B  B  U  R
S  P  S  P  C  T  E  A  C  E  A
R  E  T  L  A  L  S  O  T  A  C
R  N  N  E  L  D  M  H  E  S  S
E  C  E  R  C  P  G  N  N  R  S
T  I  D  S  U  I  W  I  I  O  E
N  L  T  T  L  M  H  A  B  S  N
I  E  E  H  A  A  H  N  A  S  I
R  R  G  R  T  C  D  R  C  I  S
P  I  K  H  O  A  U  S  E  C  U
H  E  O  N  R  L  E  L  L  S  B
R  P  A  P  E  R  C  L  I  P  S
E  T  T  R  E  D  L  O  F  E  R
```

BUSINESS CARDS	MARKER
CALCULATOR	PAPER CLIPS
CHAIR	PENCIL
COMPUTER	PRINTER
ERASER	RUBBER BANDS
FILE CABINET	RULER
FOLDER	SCISSORS
HIGHLIGHTER	STAPLER
LABEL	TAPE
LAMP	TONER

CRAFT SHOW

```
W H Q U I L T G T Y A
R E C A L I C N E T S
N M W E N O R I H N P
R I A K G S A V C I I
A M R C I C O A O O N
Y A D R R R T E R P N
I R S T I A S W C E I
T S E G O P M T B L N
I A A D A B C E D D G
B M A I I O M K T E N
I P N L L O U S L E I
H T A L S K R A O N W
X Y A A I I A B O N E
E G I G P N L O M K S
E C E E N G R A V E R
```

BASKET WEAVING	MOSAIC
COLLAGE	MURAL
CROCHET	NEEDLEPOINT
DRAW	ORIGAMI
EMBROIDERY	PAINT
ENGRAVE	QUILT
EXHIBIT	SCRAPBOOKING
KNIT	SEWING
LACE	SPINNING
LOOM	STENCIL
MACRAMÉ	YARN

EASTER

```
D Y S P E E P E Y I N
T G W S A N D D S H I
D U O I M N N H G G D
H O L I D A Y A G Y S
O S L I C C H T E E R
T E A T P A M S D D J
C B M L E S E A E E D
R E H I G N R G L C S
O I S S T A N L I O N
S B R K P G Y O O R L
S U A T C B N R B A I
B N M S E I E I D T L
U N C A K O H M R E I
N Y N M E E N C A P E
S S D H U N T E H D S
```

BASKET	HOLIDAY
BONNET	HOT CROSS BUNS
BUNNY	HUNT
CANDY	JELLY BEANS
CHICKS	LILIES
DECORATE	MARSHMALLOWS
DYES	PARADES
HAMS	PEEPS
HARD-BOILED EGGS	SPRINGTIME
HATS	TULIPS

MYSTERY LIST

Can you figure out what all these words and phrases have in common?
Read the bonus phrase in the leftover letters to see the answer.

```
P E T S R E V O A L L
A S K N I J I H L U A
L D I A T S R I F F O
M F E T C H E M G E H
N A V F T B E H T D D
U H G R Y O A E E I E
T C O N T N U R N R T
S T S R I H T G C P A
Z E C S L H U T H I E
V I T E A L G S I I F
E A U T U T T U J E E
N R S Q Q U O F A T D
R E N E P O N A C L N
H E A O O O L P K H U
A B R E T T P M U T S
```

AFGHANISTAN
CAN OPENER
CRABCAKE
DEFY
FIRST AID
HIJACK
HIJINKS
LAUGHING
OVERSTEP

PALM NUT
POP QUIZ
PRIDEFUL
STUMP
STUPOR
THIRST
TOP QUALITY
TOUGHIE
UNDEFEATED

OLD-SCHOOL FASHION

```
J O L O S A R A P D S
T H J P U Y R S A N E
E R T O P H A T O R T
L E I W D C T T H I T
D S E K I H G U S V O
R R I F S N P L N E L
I E Y N I E S U W I U
G D T L G O L E R L C
R N L R T L N D T S G
I E N O A H E O O A R
W P C S E G R T I O S
I S T A O C I T T E P
A U S E H C E E R B A
D S T E S R O C I N T
G T I U S N O I N U S
```

ASCOT
BREECHES
CORSET
CULOTTES
GAITERS
GARTER
GIRDLE
JODHPURS
PARASOL
PETTICOATS
POODLE SKIRT

SINGLET
SPATS
STAYS
SUSPENDERS
TOP HAT
TUNIC
TWIN SET
UNION SUIT
VEIL
WELLINGTONS

```
N E I T O L O B E O L
B G A B A E T Y N L W
I A M H L T U N O G R
Y P L I F T O D H Y R
S R B L O E G M P E B
S O T R O N T T E I A
M N N G I O E A L E K
B U E K A I N S E I E
B H L N S R N S T D R
A A N U A A O E N O Y
T R N T D M B L A O B
D P I J S N T R C H O
I U N G O C E H N E X
G Y O T L L U P I E S
E E L D A R C S T A C
```

APRON	KITE
BAKERY BOX	MARIONETTE
BALLOON	MOBILE
BANJO	PENDULUM
BOLO TIE	PULL TOY
BONNET	TALKING DOLL
CAT'S CRADLE	TASSEL
GUITAR	TEABAG
HARP	TIN-CAN TELEPHONE
HOODIE	YO-YO

HOW'S THE WEATHER?

```
A  D  L  Y  R  E  T  S  U  L  B
I  G  R  H  B  R  E  E  Z  Y  T
N  B  I  A  N  G  D  I  M  U  H
T  B  A  O  Z  Y  L  R  T  I  Y
W  E  S  L  A  Z  D  R  P  G  P
I  R  M  O  M  X  I  U  O  I  M
S  A  R  P  C  Y  C  L  O  N  E
T  S  A  C  E  R  O  F  B  L  T
E  E  E  E  L  R  D  Y  M  F  C
R  E  L  I  O  V  A  O  E  N  A
T  R  C  E  T  I  N  T  M  I  L
E  G  T  S  H  S  R  O  U  A  M
T  E  T  E  O  R  O  T  H  R  A
M  D  N  O  T  H  T  R  E  S  E
P  A  N  S  D  L  O  C  F  U  N
```

BALMY	FLURRIES
BLIZZARD	FORECAST
BLUSTERY	FROST
BREEZY	HUMID
CALM	METEOROLOGY
CLEAR	MONSOON
CLOUDY	RAIN
COLD SNAP	TEMPERATURE
CYCLONE	TORNADO
DEGREES	TWISTER

PHOTO FINISH

```
T Y O E V I T A G E N
U N A C G C A N M B O
A E E L A A Y K A F I
E A X M B R L C I P T
I N E P E U K L H O C
L R L L O G M T O E U
A A L E R S R I G C D
C A N O C E U A A M O
G L U D T P M R L T R
E N O T S I R T E N P
D A U S O C U R T I E
O H F A E T A O S R R
S H F O C U S P O P E
E K A T E R P B E O X
E V I T C E P S R E P
```

ALBUM
BACKGROUND
CAMERA
CLOSEUP
COLLAGE
ENLARGEMENT
EXPOSURE
FILM
FOCUS
GALLERY

IMAGE
LANDSCAPE
NEGATIVE
PERSPECTIVE
PICTURE
PORTRAIT
PRINT
REPRODUCTION
RETAKE
SHUTTER

AT THE CIRCUS

```
I  B  S  T  A  B  O  R  C  A  F
B  Y  A  W  O  H  S  E  D  I  S
O  I  U  R  W  A  E  T  N  T  T
C  T  G  T  N  Z  O  S  R  B  L
E  O  A  T  E  U  C  A  S  E  I
C  L  T  P  O  O  M  M  T  S  T
O  W  A  T  N  P  A  G  U  U  S
S  R  U  Y  O  O  G  N  N  A  U
T  V  D  L  P  N  I  I  T  L  E
U  G  I  O  O  C  R  S  P  T
M  N  E  B  P  Y  I  A  I  P  G
E  S  N  H  C  O  A  S  N  A  E
S  S  C  L  O  W  N  S  U  D  T
O  S  E  S  R  O  H  F  I  M  Y
N  A  M  G  N  O  R  T  S  L  L
```

ACROBATS
APPLAUSE
AUDIENCE
BARNUM
BIG TOP
CLOWNS
COSTUMES
COTTON CANDY
HORSES
MAGICIAN

MUSIC
POPCORN
RINGMASTER
SIDESHOW
STILTS
STRONGMAN
STUNTS
TRAMPOLINE
TRAPEZE
UNICYCLE

IT'S ELECTRIC

```
R H C T I W S E T R P
J O U L E H A X O O E
O U T L E T H T W H D
I S N C C O A E T E V
E R E Y U R R N R A O
N F C T E D E S L T E
O T S N U C N I T R Z
I H E T I O C O T I T
T G D Y N W K N C A C
A I N S A E E C S H H
L L A O C M R O A K I
U N C G A D E R V L E
S L N L O P G D U M B
N O I T C E N N O C E
I F N Y R E T T A B T
```

BATTERY	HERTZ
BLACKOUT	INCANDESCENT
CHARGER	INSULATION
CONDUCTOR	JOULE
CONNECTION	LIGHT
CURRENT	OUTLET
EXTENSION CORD	POWER
FILAMENT	SWITCH
GENERATOR	WATT
HEAT	

LET'S GET ALONG

```
S P S P L E H B E C O
U D P U L T E W O H O
S R R V P A E M I N S
N E I O T P B A W E D
E C E B C I O S M I E
S I E T N C E R S Y T
N P R E M I A H T T A
O R G E I T A I R G R
C O A H D R R O T E O
L C F O M A P R H M B
U I A O D P R T C Y A
B T N I A L E A I L L
C Y L R K G C L M L L
I O G R O U P Q U A O
S E Y T I N U M M O C
```

ACCORD	GROUP
AGREE	HARMONY
ALLY	HELP
BOND	PARTICIPATE
CAMARADERIE	RAPPORT
CLUB	RECIPROCITY
COLLABORATE	SOLIDARITY
COMBINE	SUPPORT
COMMUNITY	TEAM
CONSENSUS	TOGETHER

INSIDE OUT

Each word on the left can be placed inside one of the words on the right to form a new word or phrase, which is hidden in the grid. Can you figure out all of the new words? For a full list, see page 67.

```
Y N O T Y H C A E R P
B U E D O O I T D J I
E T W E U I A E O R N
W R M R T N R U E E E
A S A O U N R T A E T
R G E T X N E R A S F
E C R I E M E V E P R
E O C Y I S N R E T A
F I G T T P O E D S G
F W N E E F I O C A R
A E I W N K P R B N A
C T V I O C S O A A N
T N A T A R I A N T C
O R H O U R B S B E E
R L S T I B A H V E S
```

Inside Words		Outside Words	
ACT	OUR	BEE	JOEY
ASK	OWN	BET	NEST
BIT	RAG	BRIE	PAT
BOO	RAT	CAGE	PIE
EACH	TIME	CASE	PIER
EAR	TRIO	CENTER	PRY
EVENT	TUNA	FOR	RAREST
HAVING	URN	FORTE	SCREAM
INFO	WAR	FORTE	SEEN
ONE		FRANCE	
		HAS	

58 NIGHTY-NIGHT

```
D K S R E P P I L S O
C C L M A T T R E S S
N O U T S E E H S T
L L M E Y T Z T I E H
E C B F R O B E D U N
D M E B O U G D S I Q
G R R N T R Y B G I D
N A S D S B T H T W A
I L E N E B T A E O R
M A O A M L C A B L K
A R R U I S D D E L N
E B O G T Y O D D I E
R O H E D Z S T U P S
D T I R E D H A T C S
I T C Y B A L L U L H
```

ALARM CLOCK	PILLOW
BEDTIME STORY	QUIET
COMFORTABLE	SHEETS
CUDDLED	SLIPPERS
DARKNESS	SLUMBER
DOZE	SNOOZE
DREAMING	SNORE
LULLABY	TEDDY BEAR
MATTRESS	TIRED
NIGHT LIGHT	

13   OPPOSITE DAY

ANCIENT	NOISY
BLUNT	OPEN
CELLAR	PATIENT
CONSONANT	QUESTION
EXPENSIVE	REMEMBER
HORIZONTAL	STALE
INNOCENT	STUDENT
LIQUID	SUCCEED
NARROW	SUNNY
NATURAL	TALL
NEVER	

23   TWO FOR ONE

ADDITION	PRIMATE
AUDITION	PRIVATE
CARROT	SIMILE
CONCERN	SIMPLE
CONCERT	SPOIL
DAUGHTER	SPOOL
DETOUR	STATUE
DEVOUR	STATUS
LAUGHTER	SULTAN
PARROT	SUNTAN
PHEASANT	WHIMPER
PLEASANT	WHISPER

40 — NAME GAME

ANNIVERSARY	PROBLEM
AWAKEN	REINDEER
BEAGLES	RESIDENT
CHAMELEON	ROYALTY
CRAYONS	SAMPLE
DELIGHTS	SIDEBURNS
FABULOUS	SOFABED
LONDON	VEGETARIAN
MAYOR	WHALE
PLEASANT	

57 — INSIDE OUT

BASKET	JOURNEY
BEWARE	NEAREST
BROWNIE	PATRIOT
CABOOSE	PIONEER
CENTIMETER	PIRATE
COURAGE	PREACHY
FACTOR	RAINFOREST
FORTUNATE	SEVENTEEN
FRAGRANCE	SHAVING CREAM
HABITS	

1 VERY FUNNY!

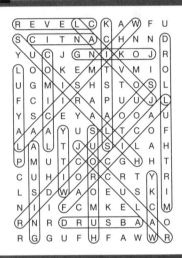

A funny joke might cause you to laugh, chortle, snicker, or guffaw.

2 AFRICA

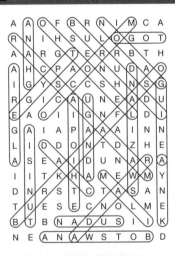

Africa is larger than China, India, and the United States combined.

3 VIDEO GAMES

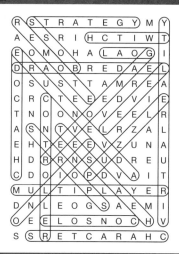

Mario has starred in over a hundred video games.

4 AT THE GYM

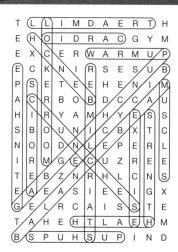

The gym exercises the body and puzzles exercise the mind.

5 SWEET STUFF

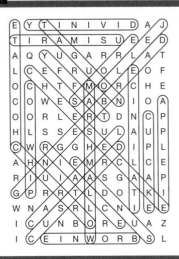

A quarter of the world's sugar is grown in Brazil.

6 UP THE MOUNTAIN

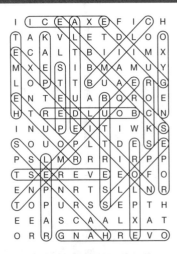

If I have to climb a mountain, I would prefer to use the escalator.

7 ENGLISH CLASS

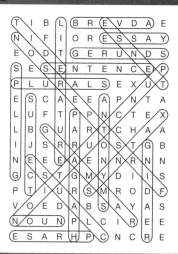

"I before E except after C" has been disproved by science.

8 LET'S MAKE A MOVIE

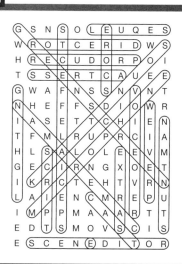

"Snow White" was the first full-length animated movie. ["Snow White and the Seven Dwarfs," to be accurate.]

9 — LA LA LA LA LA!

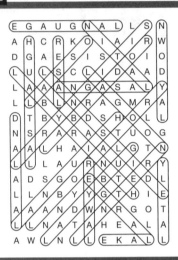

Lackadaisical lambs laugh at lads lying on the lawn.

10 — SUMMERTIME

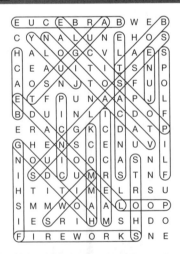

We can have a ton of fun under the sun until summer is done.

11 THE LONE STAR STATE

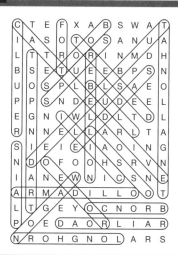

Texas was an independent nation for nine years. [From 1836 to 1845.]

12 IT'S THE LAW

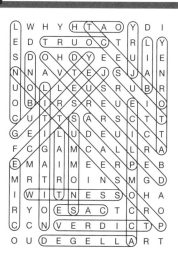

Why did the arrested farmer bring hay to court?
[He thought he had to pay "bale."]

13 — OPPOSITE DAY

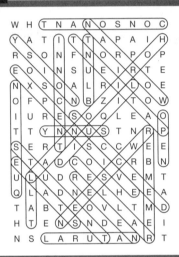

What pair of opposites are four-letter words that both end in ST? [EAST and WEST.]

14 — HAIL TO THE CHIEF

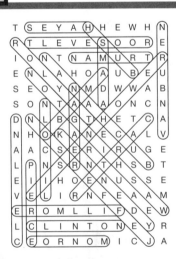

The White House was once the largest house in America.

15 PARTY FAVORS

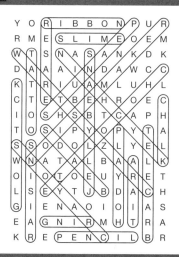

Your mom and dad will be happy about the noisemaker.

16 YELLOW THINGS

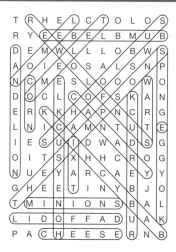

The color yellow is associated with courage in Japan.

17 — CAN DO!

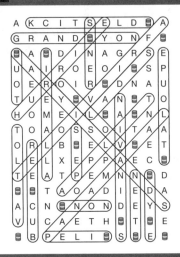

A Canada goose in a canoe cannot be expected to dance the can-can.

18 — HEY U

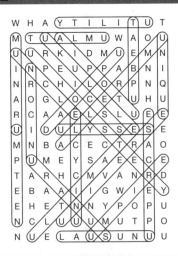

What word meaning "chase" becomes a handbag when you cut one U? [PURSUE becomes PURSE.]

19 BIG TIME

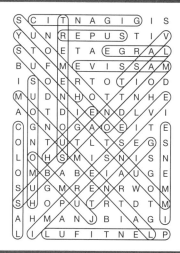

Isn't it a bit odd that "little" is a bigger word than "big"?

20 BUG TIME

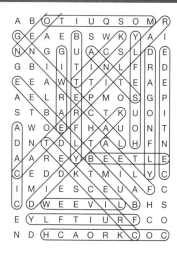

A bee's wings beat almost two hundred times each second.

21 WORLD CAPITALS

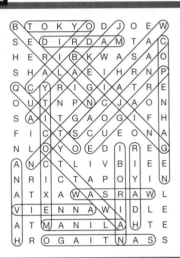

Does the Washington post office only deliver capital letters?

22 CAMPING TRIP

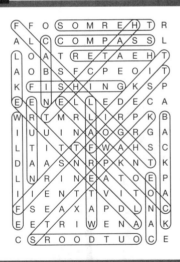

For a lot of people, camping is an in-tents experience.

23   TWO FOR ONE

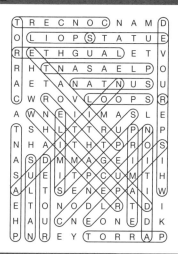

Name the two animals that end in "-onkey." [DONKEY and MONKEY.]

24   NAVAL GAZING

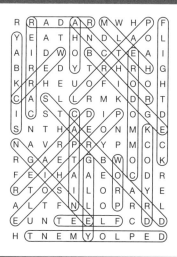

What do the folks in the Navy prefer to eat for lunch? [Submarine sandwiches.]

25 | MUSICAL INSTRUMENTS

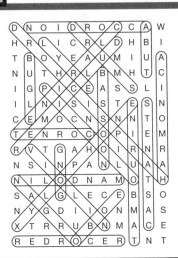

Which item in this list contains a second instrument? [BASSOON starts with BASS.]

26 | A CHEESY PUZZLE

You can tell your friends that Edam is made backwards.

27 — BODIES OF WATER

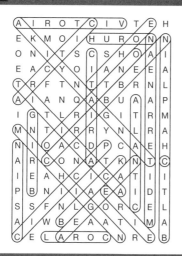

The moon's Sea of Tranquility contains no water.

28 — TRAFFIC JAM

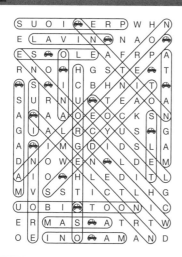

When a frog's car breaks down, does it get toad?

29 OVERWATCH

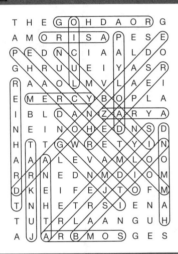

The game's dialogue is available in twelve different languages.

30 ELEGANT NIGHT OUT

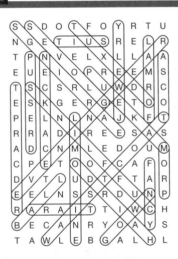

Do fortune-tellers get dressed up to attend the crystal ball?

31 · GEARS OF GOVERNMENT

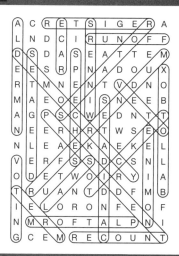

Candidates don't need new sneakers to run for office.

32 · TALENT SHOW

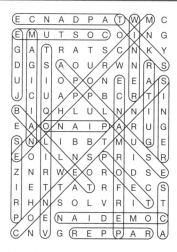

Congrats! You won a blue ribbon in word search solving.

33 PACKING LIST

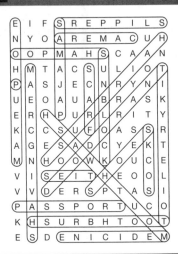

If you can't close your suitcase, you've overpacked.

34 SUIT YOU TO A T

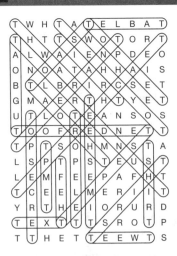

What word on this list means "small" after you drop the T's? [TWEET becomes WEE.]

35 — HOLD EVERYTHING!

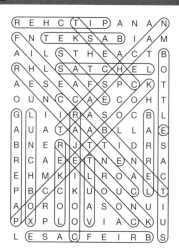

An animal that has a pouch is called a marsupial.

36 — RAINFOREST ANIMALS

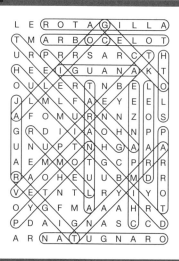

Lemurs are only found in the country of Madagascar.

37 — ALL AROUND THE TOWN

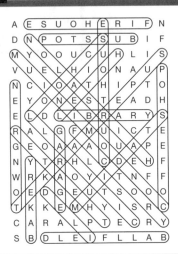

And if you live in a city, add a couple of skyscrapers.

38 — SLICES OF PI

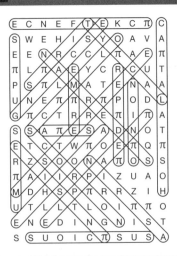

We have calculated pi to two quadrillion digits.

39 SOUTHERN FOOD

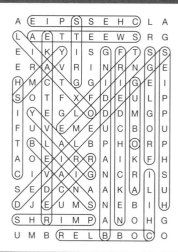

A large serving of gumbo is a jumbo gumbo.

40 NAME GAME

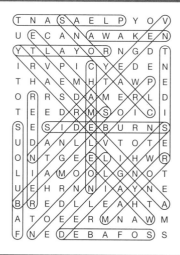

You can divide the word MELTED into two three-letter names.

41 INTO THE VOLCANO

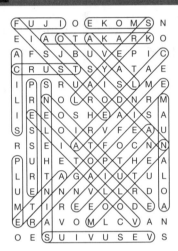

One of Jupiter's moons has over one hundred volcanoes.

42 GLASS ACT

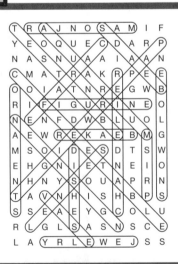

If you earn an A in making windows then you pass your glass class.

43

WOW!

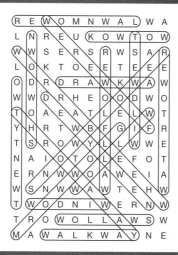

Walruses walk to the water to wait for winter to wane.

44

VISITING COLLEGES

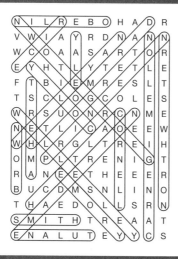

Harvard was the first college in the United States.

45 | WELCOME TO MY CASTLE

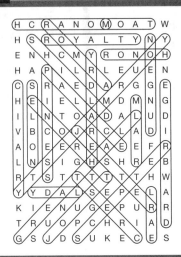

When challenged to a fight, the king put up his dukes.

46 | OFFICE SUPPLIES

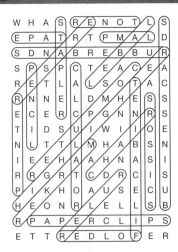

What starts and ends with E and has one letter? [An envelope.]

47 CRAFT SHOW

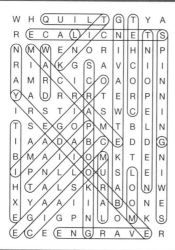

Why are origami
artists so bad at
playing poker?
[They always
fold.]

48 EASTER

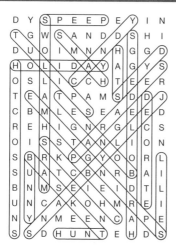

Dyeing and
hiding scrambled
eggs isn't
recommended.

49 MYSTERY LIST

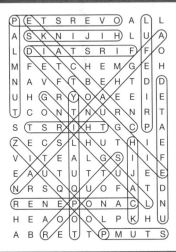

All of them have three consecutive letters of the alphabet.

50 OLD-SCHOOL FASHION

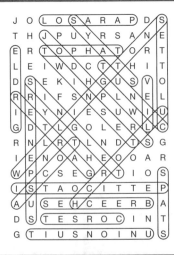

Jodhpurs are chiefly worn in horse riding.

51 THINGS WITH STRINGS

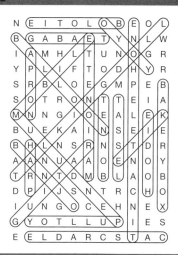

Now I'm hungry for some string beans and string cheese.

52 HOW'S THE WEATHER?

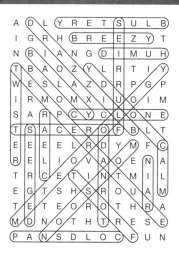

A lightning bolt is approximately five times hotter than the sun.

53 PHOTO FINISH

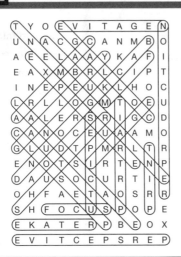

You can make a pinhole camera out of a shoebox.

54 AT THE CIRCUS

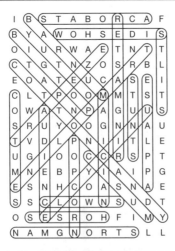

If you want to be a clown, you've got big shoes to fill.

55 IT'S ELECTRIC

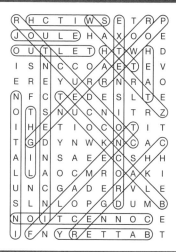

The discovery of electricity was a shocking development.

56 LET'S GET ALONG

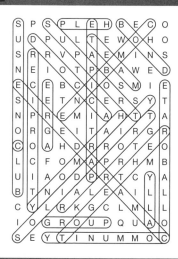

People who visit websites might form a click clique.

57 INSIDE OUT

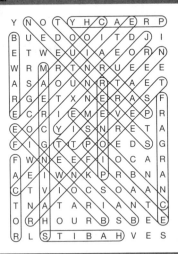

You did it! We're so excited, we can't contain ourselves!

58 NIGHTY-NIGHT

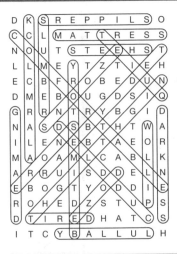

Don't let the bedbugs bite, because, boy, does that itch.